The British Museum

SO YOU THINK YOU'VE GOT IT BAD?

A KID'S LIFE IN PREHISTORIC TIMES

First published 2022 by Nosy Crow Ltd
Wheat Wharf, 27a Shad Thames,
London, SE1 2XZ, UK

Nosy Crow Eireann Ltd
44 Orchard Grove, Kenmare,
Co Kerry, V93 FY22, Ireland

www.nosycrow.com

ISBN 978 1 83994 105 4 (HB)
ISBN 978 1 83994 213 6 (PB)

Nosy Crow and associated logos are trademarks
and/or registered trademarks of Nosy Crow Ltd.

Published in collaboration with the British Museum.

Text © Chae Strathie 2022
Illustrations © Marisa Morea 2022

The right of Chae Strathie to be identified as the author and Marisa Morea
to be identified as the illustrator of this work has been asserted.

All rights reserved.

This book is sold subject to the condition that it shall not,
by way of trade or otherwise, be lent, hired out or otherwise circulated in
any form of binding or cover other than that in which it is published.
No part of this publication may be reproduced, stored in a retrieval system,
or transmitted in any form or by any means
(electronic, mechanical, photocopying, recording or otherwise)
without the prior written permission of Nosy Crow Ltd.

The publisher and copyright holders prohibit the use of either text or illustrations to develop
any generative machine learning artificial intelligence (AI) models or related technologies.

A CIP catalogue record for this book is available from the British Library.

Printed in China following rigorous ethical sourcing standards.

1 3 5 7 9 8 6 4 2 (HB)
3 5 7 9 8 6 4 (PB)

SO YOU THINK YOU'VE GOT IT BAD?

A KID'S LIFE IN PREHISTORIC TIMES

CONTENTS

WHAT IS PREHISTORY AND THE DEEP PAST?

Pages 6–9

CLOTHES AND HAIRSTYLES

Pages 10–15

THE HOME

Pages 16–21

EDUCATION AND WORK

Pages 22–27

DIET

Pages 28–33

HEALTH AND MEDICINE

Pages 34–37

GODS AND RELIGION

Pages 38–43

MYTHS AND LEGENDS

Pages 44–49

FUN AND GAMES

Pages 50–53

THE BEGINNING OF WRITTEN HISTORY

Pages 54–59

STILL THINK YOU'VE GOT IT BAD?

Pages 60–61

GLOSSARY

Pages 62–63

INDEX

Page 64

WHAT IS PREHISTORY AND THE DEEP PAST?

Imagine last week didn't happen. Or rather, it did but no one can remember it and there aren't any photos, videos or pieces of writing about it.

That would mean the really amazingly funny thing you said to your pals that made Erin Smith laugh so hard she did a **WEE** in class would be **COMPLETELY FORGOTTEN** and nobody would ever know about it!

It would also mean that the lovely artwork you made of a plastic spoon stuck to a lollipop stick and painted green would be **LOST FOREVER!** Unless, that is, it fell into a hole and was buried, and somebody dug it up and made an amazing discovery of a weird spoon-lollipop thing and it ended up in a museum.

Well, that's often all we have left from thousands of years ago.

Because there was no writing back then (only pictures), and it was a **VERY** long time ago – even older than your head teacher – not much is known about the details of these ancient people's lives.

Ooh, I got a lovely postcard from Aunt Jean!

What does it say?

Errrr... mammoth.

Almost everything we know comes from objects, skeletons and the remains of buildings that have been dug up by archaeologists.

The prehistoric period lasted for hundreds of thousands of years and is usually divided into: Palaeolithic, Mesolithic, Neolithic eras (which together are known as the Stone Age), the Bronze Age and the Iron Age. The thing is, it's not like one age stopped on a Tuesday and the next age started on a Wednesday. No, just to really confuse everyone, they all overlapped and didn't really 'begin' or 'end' – instead, they merged into one another over a very long time.

ANCIENT BONES

And while you're scratching your little hairy headbox over that, let's throw this into the mix: experts these days don't really use the word 'prehistory'. Instead, they talk about 'ancient peoples' and 'deep history'. But just to keep things nice and simple for you, let's stick to prehistoric chat for the time being.

Humans probably first came to Europe around one million years ago. Back then trains and aeroplanes were quite unreliable – you could sometimes be waiting several hundred thousand years for one to turn up – so people would have spread into new areas on foot over a very long time.

The climate during the prehistoric period played a huge part in the lives of humans. And we're not talking about a bit of drizzle meaning they had to make umbrellas out of sticks and leaves. This was **EXTREME STUFF!**

There were several Ice Ages, which left vast areas of the world covered in ice. For example, Scotland was almost permanently under a layer of ice 1.5 kilometres deep, making it uninhabitable for early humans, even if they had **REALLY** good anoraks and very big snow shovels.

When things warmed up and the ice melted, early humans returned to the areas that had been a little on the chilly side to hunt animals and forage for berries and nuts in the trees and bushes that were starting to grow again.

So, what happened? And when? And who to? For the answers to these questions wrap your peepers around THIS:

ONE MILLION – 11,000 YEARS AGO
Also known as the Palaeolithic period

This period covers a HUUUUUUGE timespan. Most of the tools used by early people who came to Britain at this time were made from strawberry jelly, which is why it's known as the Jelly Age. No, wait – stone tools in the Stone Age. Easy mistake. The climate changed over time, and during the Ice Ages it was just too chilly for humans to stay where they were, so they moved to warmer parts of the world. But people returned when things heated up again.

11,000 – 6,000 YEARS AGO
Also known as the Mesolithic period

The last Ice Age ended, and it began to warm up. People still mooched around looking for animals to spear or plants to pick, but they had to adapt to life in the forest. Lots of trees aren't really spear-friendly, so bows and arrows became the 'in' thing.

6,000 – 4,500 YEARS AGO
Also known as the Neolithic period

Farming was SO trendy. People in the Middle East started growing crops and domesticating animals, and then headed into Europe and brought their ideas with them. Sorted! Pottery began to be used for storing, cooking and eating food, which was handy as tins of soup were hard to find.

4,500 – 2,800 YEARS AGO
Also known as the Bronze Age

Things got a bit more metally at this time – although stony stuff was still around – when copper started to be used to make tools, quickly followed by bronze (a mixture of copper and tin melted together) which is harder and stronger. People began living in roundhouses and there's evidence they began fighting in battles more often, which is so unmellow. Come on guys, just hug it out, yeah?

2,800 – 1,500 YEARS AGO
Also known as the Iron Age

Guess what metal started to become the new fave? Tools and other objects were now made from iron, though bronze was still used as well. People began to live in tribes, and the Celts were the main culture in parts of Europe and Britain. The Roman Empire became more powerful as it spread across Europe towards Britain. While some people wouldn't be affected by the Romans moving in, life was about to change **BIG STYLE** for others!

2,000 YEARS AGO
Roman Britain

In AD 43, England and Wales became part of the Roman Empire as the province of Britannia. Written history properly began, and the prehistoric age came to an end. Never mind, it was around for over a million years, so it wasn't exactly a flash in the pan.

Do you ever wish . . . there was a REALLY chilly winter so you could enjoy some hardcore skating and sliding?

You'd have had no problem back in the Stone Age as there were several periods of **DEEP FREEZE!** While early humans probably rocked up in Britain a million years ago, they didn't stay put. Ice Ages meant people had to leave to find warmer places. They still had to adapt to cold temperatures, though, and coped by building shelters and learning how to hunt animals such as mammoths and woolly rhinos.

One country that was hit hard by the Ice Ages was Scotland. Much of it was covered by a thick layer of ice, with only the tallest mountain peaks poking through. With so much water stored as ice on the land and across large areas of the oceans, sea levels were much lower, so countries were much bigger – that meant the seaside was further away if you fancied a spot of sandcastle building.

But what makes Ice Ages happen? A Serbian scientist called Milutin Milankovitch came up with a theory that they are caused by a combination of changes in the shape of the Earth's orbit around the Sun and the way the earth is tilted and 'wobbles'. So if you feel the earth start to get a bit wobbly, best look for your hat and scarf!

CLOTHES AND HAIRSTYLES

Life can be SOOOO complicated sometimes. Even choosing what to wear can make your poor little brain panic.

Do you go for the clockwork musical trainers with the purple leggings and the **SPARKLY UNICORN** T-shirt or the red welly boots with the stripy yellow trousers, the neon green cardigan and the **TOP HAT**? Decisions, decisions, decisions.

But if you think *YOU'VE* **GOT IT BAD**, don't be a sillybob daftypants. At least you **HAVE** a choice. Back in the Stone Age your 'choice' was animal skins, animal skins or a tracksuit. Only joking – it was more animal skins.

Having said that, our earliest ancestors in the hot climate of Africa would have worn the grand total of **NOTHING**. Well, very little at least. And particularly if you were a child back then, you would have likely been wandering around most of the time with not even a pair of **SWIMMING TRUNKS** on to cover up!

But as early species of humans moved northwards into the colder climate of Europe and what is now Britain, they needed actual clothes to stop their **BOTTOMS** from turning into blocks of ice and falling off and **SHATTERING** on a rock.

Luckily, as time went on these folks developed special tools and weapons made from flint – more on that later – which allowed them to kill animals, then skin them and process their hide (that's their skin) to make into warm clothes. **HEY PRESTO!** Toasty bottoms all round!

They also got to grips with the skill of sewing. The Stone Agers used fibres from animal sinew (the stringy stuff that connects muscles to bones), tree bark and plants as well as grasses to bind their bits together and make them into everything from shoes and capes to trousers and hats.

When it came to showing off, people in many parts of the world would paint themselves using a red paint made from ochre.

OUCH! My new cape just bit my bum!

I'm *pretty* sure you're meant to wait until the animal is dead before you wear it.

I'm just brushing my teeth!

If they wanted to look a bit fancy, people would sometimes wear jewellery – even back in those days. The oldest-known pieces of jewellery are the perforated seashells from Blombos Cave, South Africa, which are about 75,000 years old.

Around 60–40,000 years ago in Europe, Neanderthals also wore perforated shells as ornaments, as well as using eagle claws and feathers, and painting themselves with red ochre.
Later in the Stone Age, people made necklaces and bracelets from **BONE**, **TEETH**, **BERRIES** and even **MAMMOTH TUSK**, which was either trimmed down or made for someone with a **VERY** big neck!

Do you ever wish . . .   animals were a bit more interesting?

Well, if you lived in prehistoric times you'd have had plenty of unusual, impressive and downright terrifying creatures to choose from.

There were periods between Ice Ages in Britain and Europe when elephants, hippos, rhinos and lions all wandered around, which certainly would have made the school run a bit different. And by 'run' we mean "**RUN!** There's a lion eating the lollipop man!"

When the climate turned colder, different animals would have been roaming the landscape. Mammoths would have noodled around doing mammothy things alongside woolly rhinos, wolves, bears and hyaenas, and at the end of the last Ice Age giant deer made an appearance.

Reindeer, bison and wild horses were the most important animals for humans during cold times. Eventually, around 12,000 years ago, at the end of the last Ice Age, most of these animals moved on or died out altogether. Wolves and bears still hung around forests, but the animals that remained were the ones we see today – red squirrels, red deer, hares, foxes and birds. That might not be as interesting as the Stone Age, but you're **FAR** less likely to be eaten by a squirrel than a hyaena.

As the years passed – and when we say years, we mean A LOT of years (think tens of thousands) – clothing became more sophisticated.

Bronze gradually started to be used for all kinds of things, which meant people got a whole new wardrobe . . . made entirely of bronze! Bronze sweatshirts, bronze jeans, bronze trainers – the lot. Looked great, but it was so heavy no one could move anywhere.

OK, maybe clothes **WEREN'T** made from bronze, but they had changed to some degree by the time of the Bronze Age. Animal skins and furs were still used, particularly for the likes of shoes and hats as well as leather belts, but wool and other materials were used much more often.

These shoes are GREAT! As long as I stay in exactly the same place and don't want to go anywhere at all.

If your dad went down to his local Bronze Age clothes boutique for some flash new threads, he'd probably come out with something like the following:

Come back here, sheep! I want to turn you into a pair of pants!

A sheepskin cap with the tail still attached; a cloak; a knee-length, woollen, kilt-like wrap that took ages to weave; woollen underwear (still keeping those ancient bottoms warm); deerskin shoes; and a leather belt. If he had a sword, he might have it hanging from his belt in a wooden sheath.

So, if your pop starts swanning about town with a sword and his hat goes **"BAAAA!"**, just have a quick check to make sure he's not actually a time traveller from the Bronze Age.

Baaa-ck off you baaa-d man!

As far as your mum was concerned, she'd probably be sporting a long woollen skirt and a short-sleeved blouse or tunic. She'd have a hat or a hairnet, perhaps shoes made from leather and socks to keep her tootsies warm. She might have finished off her trendy look with a leather belt, a beaded necklace, a bracelet, and possibly even earrings.

FANCY THAT!

A huge bronze dagger discovered at Oxborough in Norfolk may look deadly at first sight, but the blade is actually thick and blunt. It was probably wielded by a chieftain as part of a ceremony. So it's great to look at, but don't ask him to cut your ham and tomato sandwich into triangles or you'll be disappointed.

Rocking the woollen skirt – now for some bling!

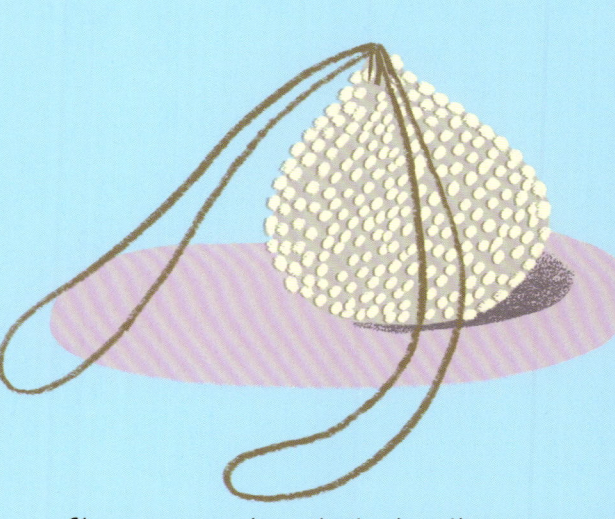

She may even have had a handbag – one was found in a grave near Leipzig in Germany that dated to between 4,500 and 4,200 BC and was covered with over 100 **DOGS' TEETH!**

My bottom is FURIOUS with this situation.

As kids, you would have worn similar clothes made from the same materials. That means very few designer T-shirts or 'wow' dresses – but you did get **ITCHY WOOLLEN PANTS!**

In the Iron Age, clothing was pretty funky.

The people who lived in western Europe and Britain at this time were known as the Celts, and **BOY** did they know how to use colour.

The three most popular colours were blue, yellow and red, and they all came from plants. The root of the madder plant produced red, woad gave blue, and yellow came from a plant called weld. After the fabric or wool was soaked in these dyes, **OLD WEE** may have been used to make the colours stick and not wash out. Pretty? Yeah, pretty **SMELLY!**

Do you like my new trousers?

Yes . . . but I'd like them a lot more if you stood MUCH further away.

In the 1st Century BC, the ancient Greek historian Diodorus Siculus, who never actually saw a Celt, told everyone in his book that "The clothing they wear is striking — shirts which have been dyed and embroidered in varied colours . . . and they wear striped coats in which are set checks, close together and of varied hues."

So they were all about **LOUD** colours and **BIG** stripes — and check out those checks!

When it came to how they'd actually put those colours and patterns to use, men wore baggy trousers called braccae, a tunic that came down to their knees with a leather belt, and then a cloak on top. Their shoes would have been made of one piece of leather tied together with a lace. Women mostly wore long, simple dresses with no sleeves, a blouse or shirt and a cape made from ox or sheepskin.

Jewellery in the Iron Age was **WELL BLING!** They had gold all over the shop, with amazing designs that included spirals and swirls and mythical beasts. One of their fave accessories was the torc, which was a thick neck-ring. Bracelets, brooches and pins for clothing were also **ULTRA-TRENDY** for the Iron Ager who wanted to make a fashion statement.

Also, your dad or grandad might well have a had an impressive moustache, although it could get in the way a bit. Old Diodorus commented, "When they are eating the moustache becomes entangled in the food, and when they are drinking the drink passes, as it were, through a sort of strainer."

Ummmm, nice work there, Dad. You appear to have a **SAUSAGE**, two **CHICKEN NUGGETS** and a blob of **MINT CHOC CHIP ICE CREAM** stuck in your 'tache!

When it came to hair, women tended to have far fewer moustaches than men, but what they **DID** have was long plaited locks and accessories like fine combs made of bone. **PLEASE** don't take that as a suggestion for something you can do with stinky old fish bones. It's not the same. Trust us.

So there you have it. If you think *YOU'VE GOT IT BAD* because you don't have a **BILLION** pairs of trainers to choose from and mummy and daddy **STILL** haven't coughed up £1,000 for that pair of electrically heated pants, at least your shoes aren't made of mammoth bits and your underwear doesn't give you a horrible scratchy **BUM RASH!**

THE HOME

Do you often have a major CRINGE-FEST about how your home smells?

There's a rich aroma of something that stinks of blue cheese and bad dreams. That's right – it's **DAD'S SOCKS**.

Or what about your brother's legendary **NUCLEAR-STRENGTH BOTTOM BURPS**?

Hang on. What's that reek? Oh, it's only Mum trying out her new organic hair dye made from **LUMPY MILK** and gherkin juice.

Well if you think *YOU'VE* **GOT IT BAD**, at least your house isn't made from **SMELLY DEAD THINGS**.

If you lived in Stone Age times your bedroom could have been made from something like deerskin stretched over some wooden poles. When we say bedroom, we mean the whole house. And when we say house, we mean a tent made from a **DEAD DEER** and some **STICKS**.

This meant the Stone Agers' home could be moved from place to place as these nomadic people travelled far and wide to hunt or gather food. They could even leave the wooden poles and just take the skin covering, so they could travel light and return to that camp at a later date.

If camping isn't your thing, how about **CAVING**? A cave is definitely less flimsy than a tent, but still short on basics like toilets, fridges and games consoles. You also might have had to share your living room with some rather gruff neighbours – **CAVE BEARS**, **CAVE LIONS** and **HYAENAS** – all of whom have a habit of eating people, which is very bad manners.

Stone Age people would have used caves to shelter and cook in. They were imaginative and told stories around the fire, made sculptures from mammoth ivory and bone, modelled clay figures of animals and people, and painted pictures on cave walls.

Do you ever wish . . . you could use something other than paper when you do art lessons in class? How about a cave? Is that different enough for ya?

Stone Age people in Europe made jewellery and sculptures from tusks and bones. That's something you can do too if your dog is happy to share its bones.

But it's the art these people made in caves, which survives to this day, that has the **WOW** factor. They created pictures of animals such as horses, reindeer, bison, mammoths and rhinos, as well as people and hands.

Kids got their hands dirty too – literally! Archaeologists think even Stone Age toddlers may have been encouraged to develop their creative skills through an ancient form of finger-painting. A well-known set of caves in France, known as the Cave of a Hundred Mammoths (which is like your bedroom being known as The Room of a Hundred Stinky Socks) contain designs called 'fluting', which is when fingers are dragged over soft red clay to produce patterns. Many of the lines were possibly made by small children – and one chamber in the cave has so many flutings made by little kids that experts reckon it may have been an area set aside just for them!

Some folk even did spray painting! Not with cans of paint, but by blowing dye through hollow wing bones from birds. Very creative . . . unless you're a bird.

Dark caves and skin tents seem almost normal compared to some Stone Age huts that have been found in Eastern Europe. They were made from . . . MAMMOTH BONES!

To build these houses, the giant jaws of the mammoth were locked together to make a low wall and the huge ribs (and sometimes tusks) were placed upright to make a dome-shaped frame that was probably covered in animal hide (skins). Why not try building your own version using bones from chicken drumsticks and banana skins? Good luck!

I'm going to go inside the bone-and-animal-skin house and you have to find me, OK?

HIDE and seek!

What do you call this new game?

If you know a friendly butcher, perhaps you could ask for some spare bones so you can start building a cool **GANG HUT** in your garden. Just watch out for hungry dogs . . .

Do you ever wish . . .
you could build a really cool gang hut?

Well, if you were around in the Orkney isles 5,000 years ago, you could have picked up some tips from ace Stone Age builders.

Nobody knew anything about the settlement of Skara Brae until a storm in 1850 battered Orkney and uncovered some amazing ruins. By the 1930s, eight homes had been excavated.

What's amazing is how complete these Stone Age joints are. They were built into the land and linked together by a series of low, covered passages – which sounds **OUTRAGEOUSLY COOL!** Imagine if you had a secret tunnel to your pal's house.

Each house has one room and contains stone furniture, including a 'dresser', perhaps for displaying special items; two box-beds; a central fireplace; and small tanks, possibly for fish bait. Next time you're having a whine-fest about how uncomfortable your mattress is, just remember it's a bit cosier than a bed made of **ROCKS!**

Various artefacts were also discovered, including tools, jewellery, mysterious carved stones and even dice! Maybe they loved a game of Stone Age Monopoly?

Skara Brae was deserted around 4,500 years ago – but nobody knows why. Some think a giant sandstorm covered the settlement, while others believe the change was more gradual. Or perhaps they just found a place with comfier beds . . .

FANCY THAT!
Dogs were common in ancient Britain, judging by gnawed bones that have been found. They would have been hunting dogs, guard dogs, sheep dogs or just pets. The oldest dogs were made of stone and were called ROCKweilers!

Houses in the Bronze Age were more permanent than skin-covered tents and less bearish than caves.

By that time, people were growing food and keeping animals on farms much more, so they had to stay put in one place rather than follow wild animals around.

Homes were usually circular with a single room and walls made from either dry stones or wattle and daub. Wattle is a panel of woven branches set between posts stuck in the ground to create a wall, while daub is a mixture of things like **ANIMAL DUNG**, clay, lime, **HORSEHAIR** or straw that is smeared over the wattle.

The doorways of many houses faced east, towards the rising sun. This would allow the dark, windowless home to be lit up naturally every morning, so no need for an alarm clock. Only problem is it's **MUCH** harder to hit the snooze button on the sun.

Your house smells weird.

Hmmm, it's either that new air freshener I just bought or the fact the walls are made from poo.

Inside, a fireplace would be the main part of the home, where all the cooking would happen, as well as providing heat and light. It's also where people would gather to share gossip, laugh and tell stories when there was nothing good on the telly.

The air would have been smoky, although most of the smoke would rise up into the roof, which was thatched with straw or turf. This had the bonus effect of killing off the creepy crawlies up there. Please **DO NOT** try this at home if you spot a tiny fly on the ceiling.

Fast forward to the Iron Age and life was becoming increasingly **FIGHTY** as tribes came to blows over good land and resources.

To keep safe, people started gathering together in or around hill forts. What is a hill fort? It's a **FORT**. On a **HILL**. Clue's in the title, folks.

These forts were usually surrounded by huge ditches and ramparts made from enormous amounts of earth piled up into mounds. These were designed to protect the people inside from attack and keep their farm animals safe. If a pig did get hurt in a battle, it would have to be taken away in a **HAMBULANCE** and given some **OINKMENT**. And yes, that joke **HAS** been around for 3,000 years.

Yoinks! Let's get out of here!

It's at times like this I REALLY wish I was a goose.

At this time, families mainly lived in round houses made from wattle and daub with thatched roofs. Meals would be cooked in a cauldron on the central fireplace, with food kept in pots around the walls.

And when it was time to turn in for the night (in the same room as everyone else, so say goodbye to privacy), you'd go to sleep in a bed made from **STRAW** covered with **ANIMAL SKINS**.

You'd have plenty of company as you nodded off – your straw and skin bed would have likely been **CRAWLING** with lots of lovely friendly **BEASTIES**! Good night, sleep tight – don't let the **BED BUGS** bite!

THE HOME

EDUCATION AND WORK

School, school, school. Lots of fun most of the time, but when it comes to certain things it can be a bit of a drag.

Like when there's been a delivery mix-up so the only thing on the school lunch menu for a whole **MONTH** is mashed liver with turnip nuggets.

Or when that new visiting music teacher arrives, and they clearly **LOVE** eating raw onions for snacks and they give you a **TERRIFYING DEATH STARE** every time you blink too loudly.

But if you think *YOU'VE* **GOT IT BAD**, then your thinks are **ALL WRONG!** Because back in prehistoric times there were **NO** schools at all, and some pretty weird stuff went down on the learning front.

Throughout the Stone and Bronze Ages, children would simply have learned how to do things from their parents, such as making tools and weapons, foraging and hunting, and preparing food and making clothes from animals and plants.

As time went on and pottery and metalwork developed, children would have been taught how to make vessels to store food in and drink from, as well as how to melt metals and make bronze from copper and tin.

That sounds super-glamorous compared with one of the other big jobs for children – **CLEARING STONES** out of fields before ploughing, then **WEEDING** and **CHASING BIRDS** away from the crops. What a **HOOT**!

Do you ever wish . . . you had a better way to travel to school than the boring old bus? A pair of custard-powered roller skates perhaps?

Well, back in the early times, the main mode of transport was a high-tech invention called 'feet'. People had to travel on foot when the climate changed, when they had to find a new home or when the animals they hunted moved on and they had to follow.

Later on, merchants would travel **THOUSANDS OF MILES** on foot to find things to buy and sell. Luckily for them, something very handy indeed was invented. You may have heard of it – it's called the **WHEEL**! To begin with, wheels were solid circles of wood and would have been attached to carts and wagons pulled by oxen or perhaps horses. But definitely not gerbils.

Humans also began making boats. The earliest types were canoes carved from single large tree trunks. The oldest discovered boat in the world is from the Netherlands and was made around 10,000 years ago – but we know that people had boats before that because it was the only way they could get to Australia, and people have been there for about 60,000 years!

By the Iron Age, transport had developed somewhat, and though jumbo jets were still a few years off, technology meant warriors could drive super-fast horse-drawn chariots into battle.

So, if you want to really impress your pals, just hook your skateboard up to a pony and you're all set!

As iron became more widely used, education began to change, too. While kids would still learn many skills and trades from their parents, new ways of learning were introduced.

For example, instead of staying with their families, it was claimed by the Roman general and emperor, Julius Caesar, that children would be sent away to learn special skills from **MYSTERIOUS** people like the Druids.

FANCY THAT!
A Druid is imagined to be a member of an elite class of priests or wise men in Celtic cultures. Very little is known about them because they didn't write down their knowledge. The only source of info about them was from Caesar and writers from the 18th Century, which means it's hard to tell what's true and what was made up. So if you're reading this and you're a Druid, please do get in touch and spill the beans. Thanks!

Children were made to learn their history, family connections, stories and verses by heart. This didn't mean reciting some **FUNNY POEMS** to make their pals giggle – we're talking super-long epic poems that would make your poor little brain go **POP**. On the good side, it saved them having to write it all down.

There was a young Druid from Wales, who ate creepy crawlies and snails . . .

That is NOT the kind of poem I was talking about!

Children could also be used as **HOSTAGES** to the Romans – but not in the way you might think. It usually seems to have involved the children of nobles rather than common people. The Romans would teach the children the way of Roman life to prepare them to lead their people under Roman rule when they got older.

If you want to try this, why not knock on the door of Buckingham Palace and ask the Queen if she'd mind giving you a few lessons on how to be all **ROYAL** and **POSH**? She's **BOUND** to say yes!

Another way kids would be separated from their families in order to be taught things was through the custom of 'fosterage'. This meant children would be sent to live with other families, where they would learn skills such as those of a warrior.

So, if you see your parents giving you **FUNNY LOOKS** and buying **WOODEN SWORDS** online, get ready to move to a new house soon.

You might not feel like getting up on a cold, wet morning to go to school and you might grumble when you get difficult homework, but at least you don't get given away to some posh Roman peeps or have to learn how to **SKIN A MAMMOTH** when you get home.

Sounds like you're a pretty lucky little chicken after all, doesn't it?

When it came to work, prehistoric kids properly had it TOUGH!

For instance, flint was one of the most important types of stone in the Stone Age, used for most of their tools and weapons. But it didn't just grow on trees – which would have been really strange. It had to be brought out of the ground.

Only problem was, very deep down in the mines, the tunnels and holes got **VERY** tight. And if an adult couldn't fit in them, who was small enough to do it? Hint: it wasn't mice with shovels.

That's right, peeps – kids had to go down into the **PITCH BLACK, DANGEROUS** mines to burrow away like moles, searching for flint.

Try to remember that next time you feel like letting out the **WHINE OF THE CENTURY** because your parents just asked you to tidy up the mouldy cereal bowls from under your bed.

If you think things got better in the Bronze Age, then write yourself a letter telling yourself to get a grip. **OF COURSE** they didn't!

Once again, when it came to squeezing into horribly small, dark copper mines, it was probably the kids who drew the short straw. It's your own fault. If you kids were 2 metres tall, it would **NEVER** have happened!

Children would also have been involved in gathering nuts and berries, harvesting crops when farming began, and cleaning up piles of **ANIMAL DUNG**.

Guess which chore I had to do today?

I don't have to guess; I can SMELL which chore you did.

So, it wasn't all excitement and glamour, you see. Nope – it was mainly hard work, with a side order of steaming poop.

Do you ever wish . . . you were allowed to drive a massive digger around?

Well, back in the Stone Age you would have been getting to grips with tools from a young age.

Flint was important as it has sharp edges, so people could use it to make knife blades, arrowheads, scrapers and axes. Pieces could also be struck together to make sparks for fire! And without that, their rhino burgers would have been totally raw. Tools were also made from polished stone, antlers and bones . . . but something big was about to happen. Metal.

People discovered how to separate copper from rock, then melted it and poured it into moulds to create tools and weapons. Then it was found that when copper was mixed with tin, it became harder and stronger. This mixture was called bronze, which was a coincidence as it was the Bronze Age. If your family could make things from metal, they could swap them for things they wanted or needed, which made them powerful.

As the Iron Age gradually emerged, people decided they'd better start making stuff from iron, or else they'd just look silly. Iron was also cheaper and stronger than bronze. And from there it was only a few thousand years before diggers were invented!

DIET

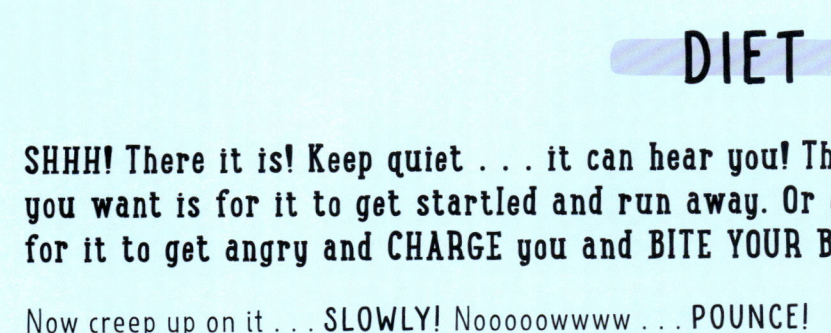

SHHH! There it is! Keep quiet . . . it can hear you! The last thing you want is for it to get startled and run away. Or even worse, for it to get angry and CHARGE you and BITE YOUR BOTTOM OFF!

Now creep up on it . . . SLOWLY! Nooooowwww . . . POUNCE! GAH! You let it get away, you tiny nincompoop! All you had to do was hunt the doughnut and catch it for your tea, and you FAILED MISERABLY!

But if you think YOU'VE GOT IT BAD, trying to catch sugary ring-shaped treats, at least doughnuts don't have ENORMOUS TUSKS to jab you with!

Back in the Ice Age periods of the Stone Age, early humans would have scavenged from the dead bodies of enormous WOOLLY MAMMOTHS for meat. If you don't know what a woolly mammoth is, imagine an elephant that's smeared itself in JAM then rolled around on a barber's shop floor until it's COVERED in hair!

It's just as well they didn't hunt mammoths – a beast *that* HUGE, with POINTY TUSKS that could grow up to four metres long, isn't something you want to get too close to.

But it wasn't the only unusual creature that would have made up the diet of humans at certain times. RHINOS, sometimes also woolly, could be on the menu, as could REINDEER (none with a red nose, so don't worry), WILD HORSES and AUROCHS, which are the ancestors of modern-day cows.

When I said I wanted to supersize my burger meal, this isn't what I had in mind.

People in the Stone Age were known as 'hunter-gatherers', which means they hunted for their meat and fish, but they also collected their fruit, nuts and herbs.

And before you ask, hunting for a burger joint and then gathering a **QUADRUPLE CHEESY MONSTER BURGER** from the drive-through does **NOT** qualify you as a hunter-gatherer.

I've no idea what they are, but they look YUMMY!

If you were a kid in those days, you'd probably be helping out with the gathering side of things while your parents and their mates went off looking for **BIG HAIRY THINGS** to chuck spears or arrows at. The hunters had to walk long distances and wait quietly for the animals – kids asking "Are we nearly there yet?" and noisy squabbles about games of 'I spy' would have scared the animals and made the hunters cross.

That's good from the point of view of not getting a tusk where you least want it, but also because the things that were gathered provided the bulk of the nutrition in the Stone Age diet, so kids helped carry out a **VERY** important job.

FANCY THAT!
Plants that would have been eaten in prehistoric times may have included chickweed, cow parsley, pignut, stinging nettle, dandelion and buttercups. Try offering your classmates a bite of your pignut and stinging nettle sandwich at breaktime and see what happens. We dare you . . .

Hooray! You hunted down the terrifying, dangerous, errr, blackberry.

For farmers, feasts were a very important part of life.

People would sometimes travel for long distances and take part in grand ceremonies, before stuffing their Stone Age faces with a **LOT** of food and drink.

At a settlement called Durrington Walls, which is two miles away from Stonehenge, more than 38,000 discarded animal bones were found – 90% from pigs, and the rest mainly from cattle. That's a **LOT** of bacon butties and beef burgers!

As there are no written records detailing what people ate, those brainy archaeologists have to use other methods of finding out info. Methods like peering at very old **POO**! Well, someone has to do it.

FANCY THAT!

Mineralised lumps of 4,000-year-old human poo found at Durrington Walls contained tiny remains of food that allowed scientists to work out what that person ate. Just think – some lucky archaeologist 4,000 years from now might dig up YOUR poo! Why not save time and take it round to your local museum NOW? (Please, PLEASE don't!)

When it came to the Bronze Age, things were slightly different. The change in climate to milder weather – think of it as the Nice Age rather than the Ice Age – meant that **MAHOOSIVE** hairy elephants and rhinos were no more.

While people still hunted, keeping animals and growing crops on farms was how they got most of their food. For your dinner you might have sat down to sheep meat, or, if you were very lucky, red deer, pike or **WILD BOAR** (hairy pigs with tusks) that had been hunted.

Birds were also popular as they were available all year round and could be caught in nets. Kind of like fishing, but drier and with slightly more feathers.

FANCY THAT!
When a body is preserved in ice or a bog, the contents of a stomach can survive. A Bronze Age man named Ötzi, whose frozen body was found in an Alpine glacier, was found to have eaten goat meat for his last meal. Obviously, his local pizza parlour must have been closed that day.

Plants and grains were a huge part of the Bronze Age diet. Porridge-type foods and barley in particular was a big deal. You'd probably end up eating so much porridge that whenever you cried, little **PORRIDGY TEARS** would ooze down your cheeks and **PLOP** onto the ground where they'd be eaten by mice.

What about drink? Fancy a nice can of cola? Well, too bad – you can have this delicious **GLOOPY, THICK BEER**, which is more like a thin porridge (yes, that again). All the family would drink it – even the children!

I'm starting to think this should be called the Porridge Age.

Once you've recovered from being **SICK**, we can move on to the Iron Age . . .

In the Iron Age, you'd mainly be eating vegetables, grains and farmed animals, such as pigs. Fish had been eaten since the Stone Age, and fish skins were even stitched together to make waterproof clothes!

You might also have dishes such as stewed hare, with wild herbs mixed in to give it more flavour and a chunk of bread on the side.

While today you might have butter on your bread, it's **VERY** unlikely it has been pulled out of a **BOG** – and if it has, you **REALLY** need to get your parents to have a word with the supermarket manager.

Forget your usual spreadables, at this time **BOG BUTTER** was a thing. It was essentially butter or other animal fat that had been crammed into a wooden container, then buried underground in soggy mud. Mmmmmm. Yummy.

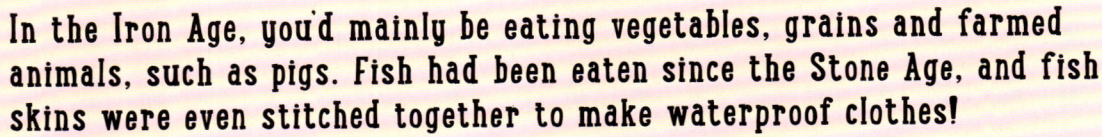

FANCY THAT!

It seems likely that bog butter was buried to stop it going off – although several thousand years might be pushing it a bit. When one archaeologist tried a 3,000-year-old bog butter he described the flavour as having "a lot of funk" with "a crazy mouldy finish". Errr, thanks but no thanks.

On the sweet side of life, Iron Agers loved a bit of honey and fruit, either fresh or dried. But there was no sugar, which meant no sticky quadruple-chocolate fudge cake topped with marshmallow, sprinkles, and cookie dough ice-cream topping. How on **EARTH** did they manage?!

Any chance you could make the first ever doughnut?

Back in those days people certainly had different tastes from us. Although they enjoyed beef, pork, and lamb just as many people do now, Ice Age people got essential vitamin C by eating the contents of **REINDEERS' STOMACHS**, which looked like cooked spinach! Feel free to stick to fruit for your vitamin C if you can't find any reindeer.

What's the secret of your fantastic health?

Lots and lots of reindeer stomach mush!

I was afraid you were going to say that.

Wondering about one type of meat that's popular nowadays, but hasn't been mentioned? Well, chickens as food weren't introduced until there was contact with the Romans. It was very un-clucky for them when they did end up on the menu.

And that terrible joke seems like a good point to end this chapter before it gets any worse.

HEALTH AND MEDICINE

There's nothing worse than getting a really annoying cold, is there?

Ok, being eaten by an **EVIL PIGEON** or accidentally falling into a paddling pool full of **COW DUNG** is worse, but you know what we mean.
One minute you're as right as rain, the next your throat feels like you've been gargling with drawing pins, there's a waterfall of green stuff flowing out of your nose and you sneeze so hard your **BRAIN** shoots out of your **BOTTOM**.
It's **SO AWFUL**! You'll definitely have to stay off school for at least a year.

But if you think *YOU'VE* GOT IT BAD, at least nobody tries to drill holes in your head to make you feel better.

Back in ancient times it seems people were occasionally subjected to **TREPANNING** – a surgical procedure during which a **HOLE** is cut or drilled in the skull.

Now, that might sound a bit extreme and painful . . .
and you're right. It **WAS**. Or at least it must have been, considering there were no modern surgical tools or, even worse, anaesthetic to ease the pain.

This procedure might have been carried out to treat epilepsy (where people have seizures) and ease headaches, although drilling a hole in your skull to sort out a headache sounds a bit like cutting your leg off to deal with an **ITCHY TOE**. Back in those days, it's likely they thought making a hole in the head would release **EVIL SPIRITS** that were causing the problems.

Not many people would have survived the hole-in-head situation – in fact, sadly for many people in history this deep, survival of ANYTHING wasn't guaranteed. Diseases, accidents and a harsh, hard life meant that the age you were expected to live to was very low compared to nowadays – just 25–40 years old.

That meant that if you were 10, you could be almost halfway through your life already. And by the time you were ready to leave school, you'd be a proper **OLD CODGER!** Although just to be clear, they didn't have schools back then.

HEALTH AND MEDICINE

I remember way back when I was nine years old.

Oh yes, and when was that?

Last week.

Many people in these times would have died as babies or in childhood, and many women would have died during childbirth, which shows how tough life would have been without doctors, nurses, medicines and hospitals.

Even if you did make it into adulthood, you'd probably end up suffering from the likes of arthritis – a disease causing painful swelling and stiffness of the joints – due to years of walking and back-breaking work. Work that probably would have begun when you were just a child.

Of course, in these far-off times, people relied a lot on plants and natural remedies to try to treat illnesses and injuries, since pharmacies were pretty scarce.

As with many things from deep and ancient history, there's not much evidence – especially when it comes to plants and the like, as almost anything natural that was used has long-since rotted away due to not being kept in a plastic tub in a fridge.

Some plants may have survived, though. Meadowsweet flowers were found in a 4,000-year-old Bronze Age grave in Scotland, for example. It's possible they were scattered there as a floral tribute, but meadowsweet does have medicinal properties, being used to treat joint aches and pains in the past. Modern-day aspirin is based on chemicals found in the plant, so perhaps those ancient peeps were on to something.

I may be dead, but my joints feel FABULOUS thanks to these meadowsweet flowers!

Archaeologists have also discovered pots containing **PIGWEED** and **HENBANE** seeds dating from about 5,000 years ago. These may have been used to treat bleeding, diarrhoea (sorry), scars and spasms. And luckily for the people back then, they weren't just for pigs and hens.

Another plant that may have been used was wild garlic, which was made into a tea as a remedy for bladder problems. It also had the benefit of making you **REEK** of garlic, which was great if you wanted to avoid getting a **CRINGE-TASTIC** kiss from an embarrassing relative.

A tea made from the tansy flower was used to get rid of **WORMS** in your guts, while the weird-sounding **FIGWORT** was used for healing cuts. Try asking for that from the school nurse next time you get a paper cut.

HEALTH AND MEDICINE

I can't run – I'm a worm!

Tansies? RUUUUN!

As far as plants are concerned some of them would have worked in treating certain illnesses, while others would have been as much use as a pair of **CHOCOLATE UNDERPANTS**.

FANCY THAT!

The teeth of prehistoric skeletons are often very worn down. This is because little bits of grit and sand were included in the flour ground on stone quernstones. Is this why we call two bits of bread and a filling a **SAND**wich? Errrr, no. It isn't. Some tooth problems would have led to infections and then . . . DEATH! Hurrah for dentists.

Must ask for less gravel and more cheese next time.

Basically, if you came down with anything nasty in prehistoric times, you could either get better due to good plants or good luck rather than any medical cures that we'd recognise. And if you were really ill, the outlook wasn't rosy.

Maybe a little cold isn't so bad after all. Just make sure you're sitting down when you sneeze so your brain doesn't get out.

GODS AND RELIGION

It can be SO upsetting when things go horribly wrong.

Like that time you swapped your packed lunch with Gary Henderson because he said he had cheese sandwiches but he totally **LIED** and gave you tuna mayo sandwiches and you'd rather eat a pair of crusty old **PANTS** than a tuna mayo sandwich.

Or the day you sneezed in assembly and accidentally did the loudest **BOTTOM BURP** in the **UNIVERSE** and got sent to the Corridor of Shame by Mrs Turbot and everyone pointed and **LAUGHED** at you.

But if you think *YOU'VE* **GOT IT BAD**, your level of 'things going wrong' is **NOTHING** compared to what kids in prehistoric times had to deal with.

And while you might make a little wish to the **GODS OF TROUSER TRUMPETING** that the school assembly scenario **NEVER** happens, folk back then took asking to be protected from bad stuff **WAY** more seriously.

Some archaeologists think Stone Age people believed animals connected them to powerful, invisible spirits that controlled nature. By painting and drawing them, and even talking, singing, and dancing for them, they could apologise for hunting, show respect, and agree how to make life better.

With this in mind, perhaps you could have a chinwag with your **PET GERBIL** so it feels respected, or apologise to a **PIG** next time you think about eating a sausage.

Archaeologists can get a glimpse of what people may have believed through objects that are found, although it's impossible to say exactly what they were for.

Several small Stone Age statues of people and animals have been dug up, for example. One of the oldest is of a man with a **LION'S HEAD** – or is it a **LION** with a **MAN'S BODY**? If any lions are reading this, that's probably what they think.

There are many sculptures and some baked clay models of women. Some are young, others are pregnant, and some are older. Discovered across Europe, they were carved between 35,000 and 20,000 years ago and may have been religious objects, perhaps made by women for their special rituals or as family emblems to bring good health and happiness.

GODS AND RELIGION

If you want archaeologists in the future to believe you were very important, simply make little clay statues of yourself and bury them. **EASY-PEASY!**

Do you ever wish . . . you gave that dead fly you found in the bathroom a grand send-off instead of flushing it down the loo? Well, prehistoric humans had various ways of dealing with the dead – and none of them involved flushing . . . or flies.

In the earlier Stone Age, people were either buried or cremated, which means their bodies were burned and turned to ash after they died. Early farmers buried their dead in mounds called 'long barrows'. A Neolithic burial site found at Belas Knap in Gloucestershire is almost as long as a football pitch and has a passageway inside leading to a set of chambers containing the bones of more than 30 people!

Some families buried important people under round mounds, until that faded out too and cremation became fashionable.

There's no sign of the skeletons of most of those who died in the time that iron use became fashionable, so whatever happened to them after they stopped being alive, it left no trace. But some people were buried carefully with things that showed their power, such as chariots or wine and oil jars imported from the Roman Empire.

One of the places where people may have come together for meetings or worship are the stone circles that can still be seen today. The most famous of these is Stonehenge.

There are around 1,000 stone circles in Britain, but what was going on at these places? There were definitely gatherings, feasting and burials of people and objects, but it's also possible that the circles were connected to worship of some kind and regarded as sacred places over the many generations they were in use.

Many of the circles are built in such a way that they are aligned to the winter and summer solstice (the shortest and longest days of the year). That and the fact the biggies took **THOUSANDS** of people **HUNDREDS** of years to build means they were super-important in a very meaningful way.

And before you ask, putting some stones in a circle in your garden is not the same thing – although do feel free to create **PEBBLEHENGE** if you feel like it. Just don't spend **HUNDREDS** of years doing it or you'll be late for school.

The people in charge of rituals and ceremonies may have been **SHAMANS**. People believed shamans could see the future and communicate with the spirits controlling nature through animals – and even become **ANIMALS!** So if you see some guy chatting to a hedgehog or suddenly changing into a **WORM**, chances are you've just seen a shaman in action!

Do you ever wish . . .
you could build something really cool in your garden?

How about a massive stone circle that takes thousands of people hundreds of years to build? Will that do? That's what a gang of people started to do 5,000 years ago.

To begin with, the circle at what would become Stonehenge, at Salisbury Plain, England, was just a round ditch inside a clay bank. Within the ditch was a ring of 56 timber or stone posts. But around 4,500 years ago, enormous stone blocks were brought in from as far off as the Preseli Hills in Wales, which are 250 kilometres away.

The largest stones weigh 25–30 tonnes, which even Big Barry Gruntpole from Class 6B probably couldn't lift. It's thought they were carried in boats and hauled over land.

To pull these stones upright, a sloping-sided hole was dug, and the rock was hauled up using ropes and a wooden A-shaped frame. The **BIG** question is, what was it for? Some think it was used to study the movements of the sun and moon, while others believe it was for funerals or that it was a place of healing. Or perhaps the Stone Age folk just **REALLY** liked circles.

Whatever it was for, there's no doubt it was an incredibly sacred, special place.

GODS AND RELIGION

Evidence for Bronze Age religion is scarce, but we know people stopped building big ritual spaces like Stonehenge - which isn't surprising, considering how much effort it took.

Around this period, people started throwing things like swords, axes, tools and even **HUMANS** into watery places like rivers, streams and bogs. It is possible that these were offerings to spirits of the earth to bring them good fortune in battle or in life.

In the Iron Age, it's likely that Celtic tribes had many gods for different things, like healing, war and crops. But different tribes would have worshipped different gods, so there were a **LOT** of gods kicking around. A proper god traffic jam.

People threw offerings such as helmets, shields, jewellery and gold coins into rivers and bogs to bring them good luck.

All of this burying and throwing of nice things is all very well, but the Romans accused the Celts of some nasty behaviour . . .

GODS AND RELIGION

According to Julius Caesar, the Celts built **WICKER MEN** (huge figures made of wicker), put people inside them and then – look away now if you get the heebie-jeebies about gory stuff – they set them on **FIRE**. That is **SO** not chill! Naughty Celts!

But Caesar never actually saw this happen. He just started it as a horrid rumour so people would like the Romans and hate the Celts. Boooo!

FANCY THAT!
The Greek historian Diodorus Siculus claimed that Celtic warriors would chop off their enemies' heads and preserve them in cedar oil to show them off. That sounds TERRIBLE . . . if it was true. Experts believe old Diodorus made up this porky pie to make himself seem civilised. Naughty boy.

What's that big hollow wicker man for?

Oh, err, why don't you pop inside to see for yourself? It has excellent central heating . . .

Do you ever wish . . . you could have more good luck? Maybe you want to ANNIHILATE the opposition at an egg-and-spoon race, or discover you'll inherit TWENTY GAZILLION pounds next Tuesday?

Well, please don't try to help the luck along by doing some of the things your ancient ancestors did. They were keen on sacrificing stuff. Sometimes it was objects such as swords and shields, while at other times they sacrificed animals . . . and even **PEOPLE!**

In many of these cases, the sacrificed people were bopped on the head, poked with sharp things or suffered other ways of not being alive any more.

As horrible as that may seem, for communities who feared bad luck it must have felt like the difference between life and death.

The Romans also claimed the Celts were big on human sacrifice. Caesar wrote that the enslaved workers of important people from Gaul (France) were burned along with the body of their master as part of his funeral. Sounds like it's much less messy to just keep your fingers crossed for good luck.

MYTHS AND LEGENDS

Hey! You! Stop wiping that under the table and PAY ATTENTION. You like stories, don't you?

There's the one your mum tells about how she met that famous band when they were just starting out and they asked her to be their singer but she said **NO** because she, like, couldn't be bothered, but she totally could have been **FAMOUS** if she'd wanted to.

Or there's your grandad's yarn about how, when he was your age, he once ate **37 CHICKEN AND GRAVY PIES** in a row and was pronounced the village Pie King and had a crown made of **PASTRY!**

These tales might be so tall that there's **SNOW** on the top of them, but if you think *YOU'VE* **GOT IT BAD**, you should hear some of the whoppers kids from the past may have been told!

While there's no way to know what stories were going around way back in deep history, the myths and legends that may have been told by Celts are better known. That's because around 1,500 years ago, hundreds of years after the Iron Age and after the Romans had eventually skedaddled, monks in places like Ireland and Wales decided to write down stories that were still told of Celtic gods, goddesses, heroes and **MAGIC**.

One Irish hero called Cú Chulainn, was the son of a god and a mortal. When he was just five years old, he defeated an enemy force of **50 WARRIORS** and while he was still a little lad, he demanded weapons from a king, but **COMPLETELY DESTROYED** 15 sets before choosing the king's own set of arms for himself.

He sounds like a proper little **BRAT!** He should have been sent to his bedroom without any porridge rather than being given a nice sword by the king.

Mind you, given how he looked, not many people would have wanted to upset little Cú Chulainn.

Loving the hair, Cú!

Yeah, just been down the salon for some new tints.

According to the legend he had **TRIPLE-COLOURED HAIR**, seven pupils in each eye and when he got annoyed one of his eyes **BULGED** out while the other sank into his cheek. Oh, and his body **ROTATED** inside his skin.

Errr, it's OK. You can have the nice shiny weapons, Mr Chulainn. Please just stop that weird body-rotating, eye-popping thing while we run away and hide behind a bush.

MYTHS AND LEGENDS

Someone who was slightly less, what can we say, TERRIFYING, was Blodeuwedd, a character from Welsh Celtic legend.

She was created from different types of flowers by two magicians, Math and Gwydion.

That sounds all lovely, but her story was pretty grim. After trying to make her husband be on the wrong side of alive (it involved a bath, a **GOAT** and a spear – don't ask), she was **CURSED** and transformed into an **OWL**, condemned to hunt alone at night for all time and ignored by the other birds.

Did you see that new owl that just moved into the forest?

Yeah, I'm not talking to her – there's something a bit cursey about her.

So if you want to avoid becoming a lonely owl you'd better behave yourself or you'll feel like a right **TWIT-TWOO**.

It wasn't just odd, magical and mythical people that the Celts were concerned with – they were into **ENCHANTED OBJECTS** as well.

For example, there's a Welsh mythical story called *The Spoils Of Annwn*, about a chappy called Arthur, who really wanted a magical cauldron. But then who **HASN'T** really wanted a magical cauldron at some point?

Of course, nowadays you just have to log on to www.magicalcauldron.com and you can get one delivered to your door the next day (if you order by 10pm).

The fancy cauldron was said to have been made of **SHIMMERING BRONZE** surrounded by **SHINING GEMS**. If you have a saucepan in your kitchen cupboard that looks like this, check to see if it's magic – you could be in for a surprise.

The thing about this cauldron is that it was pretty strong minded – it would **NEVER** provide food for a coward. Oh, and its broth was heated by the breath of **NINE MAIDENS**, something which has mainly been replaced by cookers in modern times.

Guys, can we PLEASE just pop this in the microwave?

MYTHS AND LEGENDS

Another super-duper Welsh cauldron belonged to Brân the Blessed, who was so ENORMOUS he could wade across the Irish Sea and whose head remained alive after it was cut off, which is an EXCELLENT party trick.

Hi, would you like to come to the dance with me?

Why do you ask?

Because I have NO BODY to go with!

Big Brân's cauldron had a very special ability – it could bring the dead to back to life. All you had to do was pop them in, heat them up and bingo! A pot full of ZOMBIES.

Please don't ask your dad to try this with a dead moth you found next time he's cooking spag bol. It won't go down well.

A less horrible Celtic legend concerned a young chap called Oenghus who had a dream about a beautiful girl who he fell in love with. When he woke up, he set out to find her.

The determined fellow tracked her down living by a lake. Her name was Caer Ibormeith, and she was under a **SPELL** that meant every other year she was transformed into a **SWAN**, which was a bit inconvenient. Her dad also said poor Oenghus wasn't allowed to marry her. Double bad luck!

MYTHS AND LEGENDS

So Oenghus waited until she had become a swan, then called on her. When she flapped over to see what all the fuss was about, he turned **HIMSELF** into a swan and off they flew. Just to be on the safe side they sang a spell, so that everyone below **FELL ASLEEP** and they could **ESCAPE**.

So next time you see a pair of swans eating a bit of bread at the boating pond, perhaps it could be Oenghus and Caer Ibormeith. But let's face it, it probably isn't.

After all that, your relatives' tall tales seem positively **TAME**. We'd give them 2/10 for imagination. Must try harder. Try adding a magic cauldron or two.

FANCY THAT!
In the Celtic tales of Brittany, in France, the Bugul Noz (great name or what?!) is a fairy who lives in the woods and is SO outrageously ugly that even woodland animals avoid him. Poor Bugul Noz! What you look like isn't important, Bugul. Don't pay any attention to those rotten squirrels, badgers and hedgehogs!

49

FUN AND GAMES

It's the stuff of your worst nightmares. You're just about to finish the final level of your favourite EVER video game, Stinkles the Weasel and the Bagpipes of Doom, when there's a power cut. Lights out. Console OFF!

When the electricity finally comes back on and you check your console, all of your progress has been lost. In fact, the **WHOLE GAME** has gone back to the very start. And you've been playing it since you were **TWO! GAAAGGGHHH!**

But if you think **YOU'VE GOT IT BAD**, at least you **HAVE** electricity to play cool games with. If you were a kid back in ancient times, you'd probably have been playing an exciting game of throwing a couple of **DICE** around. And no, they weren't electric dice.

Such a pair of small dice were found in the Neolithic village of Skara Brae on the Scottish island of Orkney. They would have been in use around 5,000 years ago – that's a really long time to wait for your next turn!

After a hard day's work, it must have been relaxing for families to chill out by throwing two dice around. It's likely they took turns to see who got the highest score.

If you think Stone Age dice might be made of stone, you're all kinds of wrong. They were made of **BONE!** That's like having a games console made of teeth or something – which we seriously hope you **DON'T!**

It's very hard to know what children did for fun in the Stone Age. No toys have survived, no **SKATEBOARDS CARVED OUT OF ROCK**, no **RADIO-CONTROLLED MAMMOTHS**. But it's certain that when they weren't helping with gathering food and the like, they would have been acting just like you do when you're let loose in the natural world with no mobile phones or tablets – **RUNNING AROUND, HIDING, CHASING EACH OTHER, PLAY FIGHTING, CLIMBING TREES, SWIMMING IN RIVERS AND LAKES** and all that really good fun stuff.

Wait a minute . . . the Stone Age sounds **GREAT!** Oh, hang on. You've just been eaten by a **GIANT HYAENA**. Never mind.

Fancy a game of football?

Is the ball made from a rock again?

Yes, it is.

Think I'll give it a miss, thanks.

FUN AND GAMES

The Bronze Age is also a bit of a mystery when it comes to knowing much about what children or families did for fun.

What do you want to play?

Got any good games on your tablet?

Not been invented yet.

That is SO annoying!

The lack of round things called 'wheels' was a bit of a problem back then. It made going for bike rides with your pals **REALLY** tricky and doing wheelies pretty much **IMPOSSIBLE!** Rumours of a 4,000-year-old skateboard wheel made from bronze are probably a load of old belly-button fluff.

When this thing exists, it'll be brilliant fun!

FANCY THAT!
The biggest and earliest complete wheel ever found in Britain was found in Whittlesey, in England, on the site of an ancient Bronze Age settlement. It is believed to be from a cart and is around 3,000 years old!

As time rolled on and iron tools and weapons became a thing, a little more comes into view...

For instance, glass gaming pieces have been found in Iron Age graves – and where there's gaming pieces, there have to be **GAMES**. What those games were isn't known, but they could have been some form of board games. Which means that there were almost certainly **MASSIVE ARGUMENTS** happening in roundhouses because Cynwrig accused Nechtan of cheating by hiding some glass gaming pieces inside his woollen underpants, which is **SO UNFAIR!**

Small discs, like games counters, have also been found on Orkney. It's thought they could belong to types of board games archaeologists don't yet know about.

FANCY THAT!

A game found in an Iron Age grave in Stanway, England, consists of 26 blue and white glass counters and a chequered board. There were no dice, which means it was probably a game of strategy. There were also no controllers, chargers or plugs due to a rather inconvenient lack of electricity.

Aside from the whole 'hanging out with the fam by the fireside playing games' thing, kids probably would have enjoyed pastimes such as practising their target skills with **SLINGSHOTS** or fighting with **WOODEN SWORDS**, perhaps one day dreaming about becoming warriors.

So if you ever get so **UNBELIEVABLY** bored that your brain jumps out of your earhole and runs off down the street, just take a moment to remember how incredibly **LUCKY** you are that you have wheels, electricity and billionty-hundred gadgets to choose from!

THE BEGINNING OF WRITTEN HISTORY

Oooooh, it's SO annoying when your classmates find out a VERY IMPORTANT SECRET that you've been trying to hide from them.

You'd wrapped your packed lunch box in 17 layers of tinfoil and sprayed it with your dad's most EYE-WATERING aftershave just to mask the lovely aroma. But it hadn't worked.

That's right, they've discovered that you have one of your mum's famous marshmallow and fudge chocolate brownies.

And what do your friends do when they make this AMAZINGLY AWESOME discovery? They INVADE your lunchbox of course. And all you're left with are crumbs and memories.

But if you think YOU'VE GOT IT BAD, at least your lunchbox hasn't been invaded by an all-powerful army of sword and spear-wielding Roman warriors! Unless they REALLY like your mum's brownies and have a very spacious time machine.

So this is the bit where this part of deep history, aka prehistoric times, comes to an end and for some people written history starts.

FANCY THAT!

It was said that when Emperor Caligula attempted to invade Britain in 40 AD his army was set to cross the English Channel when he changed his mind and ordered his soldiers to collect seashells instead! He sent them back to Rome and claimed he had conquered the ocean. Just to be clear, picking up a couple of whelks and a cockle does NOT mean you own the sea.

You see, while the Romans brought much suffering to the lands they invaded, by way of their habit of poking people with SHARP THINGS until they were slightly on the dead side, they also brought written language and recorded what was going on.

And so history was born. Awwww – ickle baby history. Sweet.

But why did the Romans, under their emperor, Julius Caesar, decide to attack and conquer Britain 2,000 years ago? Simple – they thought Britain had gold, silver, lead, copper and tin, and they wanted it.

It didn't go well to begin with. In 55 BC old Julius tried to invade Britain, but the local warriors weren't having any of it. The next year he tried again but **STILL** had no luck. In fact, it wasn't until almost **100 YEARS LATER**, in AD 43, that the Roman general Agricola, under the command of the Emperor Claudius, finally conquered Britain. Third time lucky (unless you were an Iron Age Briton, that is).

FANCY THAT!

When General Agricola, under the orders of Emperor Claudius, finally succeeded in invading Britain, his army used fancy new weapons, like huge catapults called ballistas. Apparently, Claudius even rocked up with a load of war elephants! With creatures like that on his side, conquering the island must have been a much easier TUSK!

THE BEGINNING OF WRITTEN HISTORY

With the Romans being pretty wordy characters, their records provide the first written history of the Celts of Britain.

Joolz Caesar said the Britons were fearsome warriors who charged into battle on chariots. He wrote, "All the Britons paint themselves with woad (dye made from a flower), which produces a dark blue colour, and for this reason they are much more frightful in appearance in battle."

So if your dad appeared looking like a **FREAKY BLUE ALIEN**, it probably meant he was off to do a spot of battling.

If you want to shake up the opposition at your next school netball match, simply grab some blue paint and get all Celtic on your face.

It certainly wasn't a game for kids back in those days, though. In AD 43, a huge Roman army arrived in Kent and battled their way inland from the beach. Anyone who stood in its way as they smashed through hillforts and villages was for the **CHOP**. For children, it must have been terrifying.

While some tribes fought back, others decided it would be better (and less choppy) to make peace with the Romans. If they did so, they had to obey Roman laws and pay taxes.

One Celtic queen called Boudica got fed up with having to give up land and pay the Romans, so she got a big army together and went off to do some very naughty things to Roman towns, such as **BURNING THEM TO THE GROUND**.

Do you ever wish . . . your mum was a bit fiercer?

Sure, she's really lovely and she smells of custard creams – but wouldn't it be cool if she occasionally surprised everyone with something wild and unpredictable? Well, if Boudica was your mum, you wouldn't be complaining about her being boring.

In the late Iron Age, Boudica was queen of the Iceni people of Eastern England. Her husband, Prasutagus, was the top guy when the Romans invaded in AD 43, and they allowed him to continue to rule. But when he died, those naughty Romans took the property of the Iceni and are also said to have flogged Boudica and treated her daughters terribly.

Boudica was **FURIOUS** and rose up in rebellion against the Romans in AD 60-61. She united many Celtic tribes and, with her army of tens of thousands of warriors, inflicted a surprise defeat on the Roman Ninth Legion. She then went on to destroy Colchester (the capital of Roman Britain) as well as London and Verulamium (St Albans), killing thousands in the process.

Finally, Boudica was defeated by the Romans at the Battle of Watling Street and it is believed that, to avoid being captured, Boudica poisoned herself. On second thoughts, perhaps it's best if your mum sticks to being lovely . . .

As the Romans battled further north and west, they encountered stiff resistance from the locals in places like Wales and Scotland, but eventually much of the southern half and the east of Britain became very Romanised.

British people who had once lived as Celts changed pretty quickly to the Roman way of life. Towns were redesigned to a Roman-style grid-system of streets and grand public buildings were built. What had been Iron Age tribal settlements now had forums (market squares), basilicas (assembly rooms), temples, theatres, bathhouses, amphitheatres and even hotels and shopping malls! Just the place to buy the latest Roman fashions from Togas-R-Us.

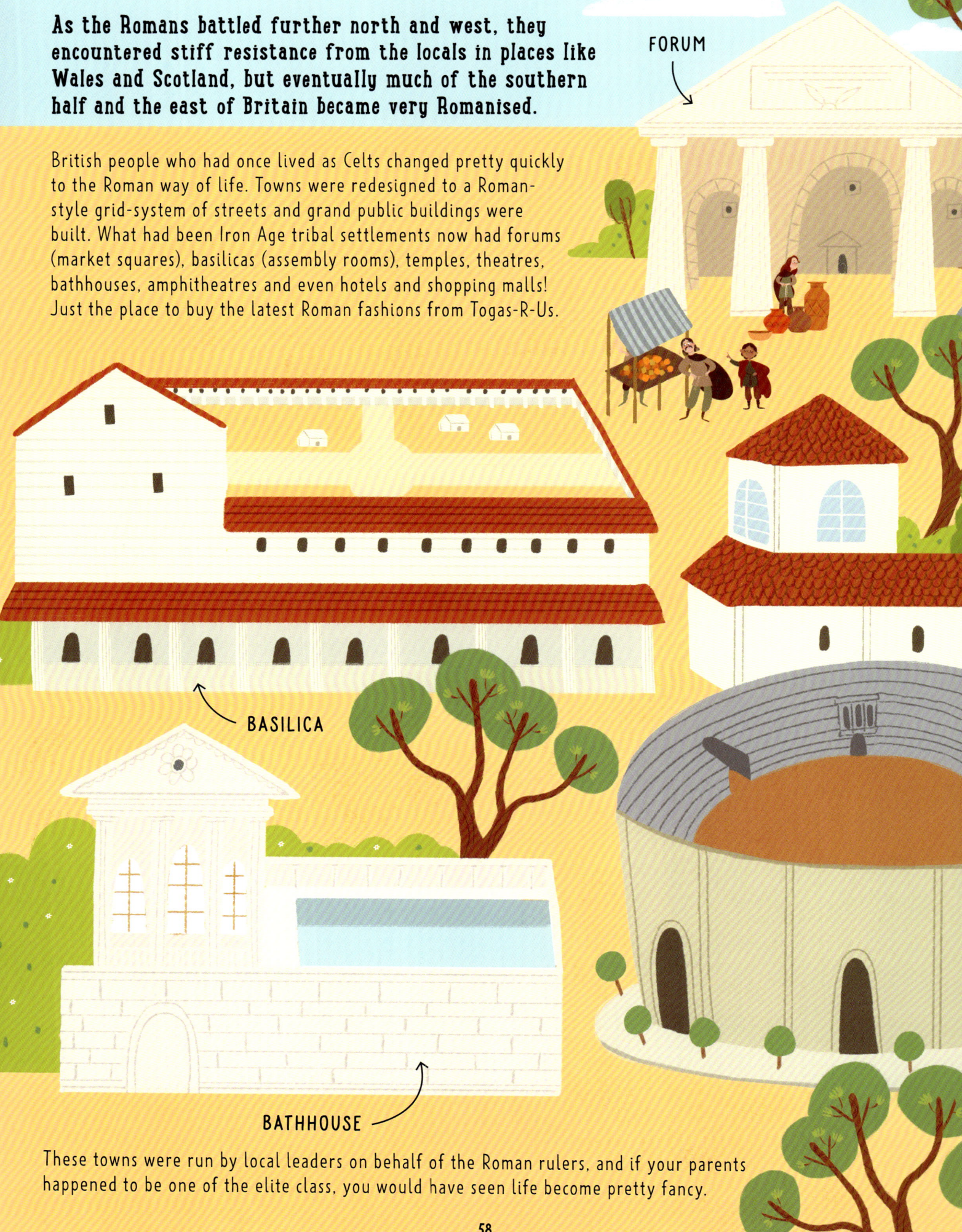

FORUM

BASILICA

BATHHOUSE

These towns were run by local leaders on behalf of the Roman rulers, and if your parents happened to be one of the elite class, you would have seen life become pretty fancy.

No more of Dad smearing himself in blue gunk – your parents would have been sipping French wine and eating fish sauce from Spain while enjoying hearing Greek myths. And you would probably have lived in a swanky townhouse or, even more posh, a villa in the country, complete with stunning floor mosaics, frescoes painted on the walls and beautiful pottery on display.

TOWNHOUSE

At last – we have writing! Now people can write really AMAZING books about our lives 2,000 years from now!

TEMPLE

I hope we get a mention in it!

VILLA

AMPHITHEATRE

Unlike deep history when nothing was recorded, details of life under Roman rule and beyond were now written down.

History had begun – and it's still going on now.

That's right . . . **YOU'RE HISTORY!**

THE BEGINNING OF WRITTEN HISTORY

STILL THINK YOU'VE GOT IT BAD?

So here we are at the end of the book.

Awwww. There, there. No need to cry. OK, perhaps you can cry a little bit. After all, it was a **VERY** good book, wasn't it?

But rather than leaking water out of your eyeholes, you should be laughing and singing and doing a weird little dance. Because compared to those poor kids from the deep past, you don't have it bad **AT ALL**.

Obviously, you might have tough times too. Like when your butler – sorry, dad – makes your orange squash just a teensy-weensy bit too weak. Simply unbearable.

But by and large you have it pretty good in comparison.

Let's just check the evidence.

Do you . . .

1. Have to take a different route to school every day to avoid packs of giant wild hyaenas? **YES/NO**

STILL THINK YOU'VE GOT IT BAD?

2. Feel you have to throw a sword in a pond before you buy a raffle ticket at the school fair to try to make sure you win? YES/NO

3. Have to choose between a woolly mammoth pie and a bog butter sandwich for lunch every day at school? YES/NO

"Hello, what seems to be the problem?"

"It's my butter, it's just not BOGGY enough."

If you answered mainly NO, then congratulations – life is relatively good, and you can proudly wear a T-shirt that says: 'I have it better than a prehistoric kid'.

If you answered mainly YES, then you need to have a SERIOUS talk with your parents about moving to a new era as soon as possible – you may accidentally be living several thousand years ago.

But let's face it, chances are you haven't got it as bad as kids back then.
So say a quick "HURRAH!" and stop that grumbling.

GLOSSARY

So there you have it! You've read the book, you've marvelled at the pictures, you've laughed at the jokes and you've stuffed your tiny **BRAINBAG** so full of fabulous facts that it is now the size of a **BEACH BALL**! But what's that we hear you cry? You want more? **MORE?!** Why of **COURSE** you can have more!

The thing about a book filled to bursting with words is that you might not know what all of them mean. But don't worry – and don't be embarrassed – because we're here to help by filling in any gaps that you might have on the word front.

So relax, sit down, take off that **RIDICULOUS** glow-in-the-dark hat and check out our explanation of some of the words that may have gone in through your little eyeholes while you were reading . . .

AMPHITHEATRE

When the Romans conquered Iron Age Europe and Britain, they built many amphitheatres, which are huge, circular or oval, open-air entertainment venues that could hold thousands of spectators. They were used for gladiator fights, executions, and religious festivities. So kind of like a football stadium, but with slightly more blood and death.

ARCHAEOLOGIST

Is your favourite toy a spade? Do you like poking around in your macaroni cheese in the hope you'll find something interesting? Then you should become an archaeologist! That's the name for someone who studies human history by digging up the ground in ancient sites and analysing the objects and remains they find there. Ideal for nosy peeps with trowels!

BOG

A bog is a soggy area of spongy ground that is mainly made of decaying plant matter called peat. The water in bogs is brown and if you were to go for a walk in a bog, you'd probably sink pretty quickly – so DON'T! Many of the preserved ancient bodies that have been studied were discovered in bogs, so we should be grateful for them. Thanks, bogs!

CAULDRON

You might think only witches use cauldrons, but normal folk used them all the time from the Bronze Age onwards. They were used to cook broths and stew in, and they could be ENORMOUS! They also had a magical role in Celtic myths and legends. Certainly more interesting than your average microwaveable bowl.

DOMESTICATED

When animals were domesticated by early humans, it meant people tamed them to use as a pet or on a farm. Wolves became dogs for hunting or just enjoying, while wild horses and pigs were tamed to use to pull carts or eat. If you're a bit wild sometimes, perhaps you could do with a little domestication . . . though hopefully not on a farm!

FORAGE

In the days when people were hunter-gatherers, they would forage for food. That meant they would go from place to place searching for nuts, berries, plants and herbs to eat. You might forage in shops for fizzy sweets that turn your tongue blue but trust us – it's not the same thing.

FRESCO

The insides of Roman villas were often decorated with frescoes. That means that, when still damp, the fresh plaster on the walls was painted with watercolour paints. Many different scenes were created, from landscapes to people to gods. Note: drawing on your bedroom walls with permanent marker is NOT creating a fresco.

GAUL

Gaul was an area of western Europe that covered what is now modern-day France and parts of Belgium, the Netherlands, Switzerland, western Germany, and northern Italy. It was inhabited by Celtic tribes and was invaded and conquered by the Romans just over 2,000 years ago. Those Romans just LOVED a bit of invading and conquering!

LONG BARROW

Long barrows are ancient stone monuments to the dead. They are made of elongated mounds of stone containing a passage and chambers, which hold the bones of between five and 50 men, women, and children. If you have a long barrow in your garden shed, it's hopefully for moving earth and leaves and does NOT contain 50 skeletons!

MINERALISED

Archaeologists have managed to find out interesting things about ancient diet and disease by studying lumps of mineralised poo called copralites. Mineralisation is what happens when organic matter (poo, leaves, wood, etc.) becomes hard and like stone over time. It's SO exciting that your poo could become an important fossil in a few thousand years' time.

MORTAL

In ancient cultures around the world, beings were separated into gods and mortals. Mortals were normal humans with no special powers, unlike gods. No offence intended, but you are a mortal . . . unless you are keeping a VERY cool secret.

NOMADIC

People who are nomadic travel around from one area to another and don't have a settled home. In prehistoric times, Stone Age hunter-gatherers were nomadic so they could follow the animals they ate or find other food. Going on nice summer holidays in a caravan means you're lucky, not nomadic.

QUERN

A quern was a type of hand-operated mill used for grinding corn. It was made of two circular stones, with the top one being rotated to turn grain into flour for making bread. Bits of sand and grit would come off the stones and end up in the bread, which wore down people's gnashers and brings a whole new meaning to the term "through gritted teeth".

RITUAL

Religious life in ancient times would often involve rituals, which are ceremonies during which people did or said certain things in a certain order. It was very important to people that they got them right, as they believed rituals could affect their lives very deeply. Practical jokes involving whoopee cushions were frowned upon.

SOLSTICE

The solstices are the longest and shortest days of the year. In the northern half of the Earth, the winter solstice happens when the North Pole is tilted farthest from the sun. When the North Pole is tilted towards the sun, that's the summer solstice. It has to happen on a planetary scale though – simply tilting yourself towards or away from the sun won't make the day longer or shorter.

SUPERNATURAL

Powers beyond nature, like fairies and spirits, have always been an important part of belief. When something is supernatural it means it comes from an unseen force that falls outside the laws of nature or scientific understanding. Your best pal's bottom burps after a large helping of cauliflower cheese may fall into this category.

INDEX

Agricola 55
Amphitheatre 59
Animals 11, 16-17, 28, 30-31
Archaeologist 6, 17, 30, 36, 38-39, 53
Art 6, 17, 38
Basilica 59
Bathhouse 58
Blodeuwedd 46
Boat 23
Boudica 57
Brân the Blessed 48
Britannia - see Roman Britain
Bronze Age 6, 8, 12, 20, 22, 26-27, 30-31, 36, 42, 52
Caesar 24, 43, 55
Caligula 54
Cave art 17, 38
Celtics 44-49, 57
Celts - see Celtics
Claudius 55
Climate 7-8, 10-11, 23, 30
Clothing 10-15
Cú Chulainn 44-45
Disease 35
Dogs 17, 19
Druid(s) 24
Dye 14, 16-17, 56
Farming 8, 20, 27, 30, 39
Fire 20-21
Flint 11, 26-27
Food 20-21, 28-33

Foraging 7, 22, 29
Fosterage 25
Frescoes 59
Games 50-53
Gods 38-43
Hill fort 21
Home 16-17
Hunter-gatherers 29
Hunting 7, 22, 29
Ice Age 7-9, 11, 28
Iron Age 6, 9, 14-15, 21, 23, 27, 32-33, 42, 53, 55, 57
Jewellery 11, 13, 15, 17, 19
Legends - see Myths and Legends
Mammoth 9, 11, 18, 28
Medicine 34-37
Mesolithic 6, 8
Myths and Legends 44-49
Neanderthal 11
Neolithic 6, 8, 39, 50
Ochre 11
Oenghus 49
Palaeolithic 6, 8
Pictures 6
Pottery 8, 23, 59
Priest 24
Religion 38-43
Roman Britain 9, 54-59
Roman Empire 9, 25, 39, 42-43, 54-59
Roundhouse 21
Science 9

Skeleton(s) 6, 39
Solstice 40
Stone Age 6, 8, 10-11, 16-19, 22, 26-30, 38-41, 50-51
Stonehenge 40-41
Tools, 7, 11, 19, 22
Townhouse 59
Travel 7-8, 23
Tribe(s) 9, 21, 42, 57
Wattle 20
Weapons 11, 22, 25-27, 44-45
Wicker men 43
Work 26-27
Writing 6